Job Hunting?

Plan
for Success

Catherine Middleton

DISCLAIMER

No liability for the contents of this book can be accepted. Use the concepts, examples and other content entirely at your own risk. As this is a new edition, there may be inaccuracies as new technologies and information can change over time.

ISBN-13: 978-1539074335

DEDICATION

For Jobseekers who need support in
Planning to be Successful

CONTENTS

CHAPTER ONE

THE FIRST RUNG

One wonders with the unemployment situation the way it is, how on earth job seekers are going to find their way into employment opportunities, to perhaps commence or recommence what is hoped, will be a rewarding job opportunity.

Although today's employment environment is tight it is not impenetrable, there are opportunities for people with the 'right' attitude. So what is the **'RIGHT ATTITUDE?'**

Companies can often take on new staff with a view to train and nurture their progress through the initial period of their appointment. They recognize that applicants may not have the level of experience required, but just as important is a willingness on the part of the new employee to become part of a team and have a '**can do'** attitude. It is a two-way contract with both parties benefiting, the new employee from being offered an opportunity to join a company, and the company who is able to offer training into their way of doing business, a win:win situation.

As a person looking for employment, the initial step of gaining a position can be difficult, but going through the process of applying for positions, and attending interviews, eventually builds confidence.

If we look at a career as rungs on a ladder, it is easy to see that starting on the first rung, having taken on board an opportunity to get into the workforce, is the first step in climbing that ladder; thereafter working the way up one rung at a time, to where a person may themselves in say five years' time.

If you ask any high profile person how they started their career, you may be amazed at some of their responses. There are few if any, that have an opportunity to start at the top, it is more evident that they commenced on the first rung, learnt the business and then steadily progressed to where their aspirations saw them heading.

Getting into the workforce is not something to be taken lightly, it needs a well thought out plan of attack, and this handbook will be your 'right hand' reference to working through the process. Each chapter will give you an insight into the realms of recruitment and selection that are clear, up to date and can easily be implemented into your own 'getting a job' process

USE THIS PAGE TO MAKE NOTATIONS

CHAPTER TWO

WHAT DOES AN

EMPLOYER LOOK FOR?

According to the Federal Government Australian Jobs 2015 report, employers are looking for three main characteristics:

1. **A positive 'can do' attitude**

   This means that when asked to undertake a job, even if that job appears menial or 'not relevant' to them, someone who says "YES, I can do that", is someone who will be well thought of by an employer, and will be considered to be a 'team player'.

2. **A willingness to learn and participate in entry-level jobs**

   You will have heard the phrase, 'you need to learn to walk before you can run', this is particularly relevant when starting your first job. Being willing to learn the basics of any role will strengthen your knowledge of the job and of the company. This is invaluable as you climb the ladder and take on other responsibilities.

3. **Volunteers for tasks to gain experience and work skills**

   Again, a terrific attribute for any newly appointed employee. It is amazing what you learn when volunteering, the people you meet, creating more connections across an organization, and again the knowledge you accumulate is invaluable.

The report also outlines more general attributes sought by employers, reflecting on the personality of applicants as new recruits.

a. **Honesty and Integrity**

   Goes without saying that these are essential attributes for any employee. In the business world, being honest and displaying integrity in all interactions and dealings, is paramount to the credibility of not only the employee, but also the business that employs them.

b. **Is well presented**

   This is a big issue, as personal presentation appears to be less important than in earlier years. When it comes to presenting oneself for interview, personal appearance is top of the list of consideration when candidates are assessed.

The person or persons interviewing a number of candidates, gets perhaps ½ hour to make an assessment which will include how the candidate presents themselves, how they speak when greeted, and their personal appearance.

Personal appearance includes:

✓ Clothes are clean, neat and appropriate. No torn jeans (although in fashion at the moment, are not considered acceptable). Have a look at what others are wearing at the company you are aiming at, and see what the standards are.

✓ Shoes should be clean and again appropriate (no stilettos, sneakers or thongs).

✓ Hair should be clean and combed. (Although it may appear acceptable to have hair pulled back with a band and not combed), from a business perspective, it may not give the professional image the employer is looking for.

✓ Hands and fingernails should be clean.

✓ Makeup should be minimal, and no heavy perfume.

✓ No large dangling earrings or bracelets that make a noise when you move.

All of these protocols may seem like a personal attack on your individuality, but if you are serious about becoming part of the workforce, you need to make a good impression at your interview. As previously advised, interviewers make their initial assessment within the first 60 seconds of you entering the room, even before you begin to speak, so ensure your appearance reflects the position you are seeking. 'Dress for Success', which means at interview you should dress for the position you see yourself in, not where you are now.

Having sat on many an interview panels, I understand what companies are looking for in the candidates they see, and I can assure you that these points are the essentials of personal presentation.

c. Is Reliable

Reliability on the day of interview is demonstrated by turning up on time, at the right place, with the right paperwork in your hand.

At interview your general reliability could be demonstrated by relating a personal achievement where reliability had contributed to your success in a certain situation.

d. Speaks with clarity

Communication skills are a must in any workplace situation. It doesn't mean that you have to be the life of the party, but it is essential that you can clearly articulate when in conversation with someone. This skill will be tested at an interview, as it is the one time when you need to 'sell' yourself. This means you have to be able to tell the interview panel about yourself, clearly and concisely.

It is perhaps a skill that is not so prominent in todays' society due to 'texting', emails and other non-verbal communication. It would therefore be a good idea to get some practice by role playing an interview with perhaps a relative or friend who can give you constructive feedback.

TIP: It appears that the word 'Like' has invaded conversations, to the point that it occurs more than once in any one sentence. As it does not add 'value' to a conversation, it would be appropriate not to use it at an Interview. It may confuse the message you are trying to give to the person interviewing.

e. Has enthusiasm

This is a great attribute to be able to demonstrate at an interview. Enthusiasm shows itself in a person's face, when they speak, and even in their mannerisms. It is a bit like passion, if you have a passion for a particular hobby, book or career, it will come out in what you say and how you say it.

f. Someone who is motivated

Think about what motivates you. Analyze why and how it changes the way you think or act. If you are applying for a position that inspires you, then tell the interviewer why.

g. Competence

You will need to indicate some level of competence to undertake the position applied for.

A Candidate's level of competence may be virtually none existent when applying for a first job straight out of school, or returning to the workforce after a period of unemployment. It doesn't mean however that you aren't interested in the type of business, or the particular type of work. You may have undertaken a particular study course or have a 'life' experience that has given you a strong interest in this position. You may also be able to display a level of competence in another area which indicates your competence to successfully complete tasks at an appropriate level.

h. Energy, Ideas & Enthusiasm

As stated earlier, if you have a passion for a certain industry, it would be considered a positive attribute by any interviewing panel.

Consider what Kevin Rudd, said in a speech he gave when appointed Prime Minister, *"Young people, we need your energy, your ideas and your enthusiasm. We need you to support us to meet the great challenges ahead".*

It is common sense to say then that the Youth of today, are very much the citizens of tomorrow, and if Australia is to continue to prosper, this country needs all the energies, ideas and enthusiasm that this next generation brings to the table.

NOTES PAGE

CHAPTER THREE

COMPILING

YOUR RESUME

A professional looking Resume is the key to getting a potential recruiter to look past the first page. Whether it is a recruitment agency or the Human Resources (HR) department of a company, they may receive hundreds of resumes either over their desk or by email every week, especially when a position is advertised. To ensure that your resume gets noticed, there are a few design issues you should be aware of. Example Resume Template on page 15, which can be used to create your own document.

✓ Use a an easy to read font - eg Arial 11 or 12 point.

✓ Use a Word document, inserting a 'table' so that inputting your information is as easy as tabbing from one cell to the next.

✓ Insert a Header showing your name and contact mobile number on the right hand margin.

✓ Insert a Footer and insert page numbers ie Page 1 of 3 (set auto page numbering). (This will assist the reader to keep all papers together and know how to contact you quickly).

In the content of your Resume use the following headings:

✓ **Name / Address / Contact** number (Mobile is best where they can leave a message if you are unavailable to take the call)

✓ **Education & Qualifications**

✓ **Goals** – not essential, though it does add value to say what you want to achieve, or what you aspire to.

✓ **References** – show contact details of referees. Ensure you have asked each one's permission before adding their details.

✓ **Work History /Work Experience -** commencing with the current situation. State details of relevant experiences you may have had over the past year which will compliment your application for any specific role.

✓ **Photo** - Although not compulsory, you may like to add a photo to the front page, as it assists in recalling who has been interviewed. This is very handy to have when multiple candidates are interviewed on the one day. A professionally taken photo will enhance the professional image you want to portray.

When your document is complete, ensure you proof read it, and undertake a spell check. This is a **professional** document, and must look that way.

Be honest in your statements. Overstating your experiences will trip you up at interview. Remember earlier we talked about Honesty and Integrity, these attributes are essential in any dealing you have with a potential employer.

They will understand that you will have limited experience, and so will be looking for a related level of competence. You can relate being part of a team, or successful completing a project, these experiences will carry weight when applicants are being shortlisted for interview.

PHOTO

1st page include:

NAME:

ADDRESS: (*It would be acceptable to just name your suburb*)

CONTACT No: (*Mobile phone is best, as they can leave a message*)

GOALS:

EXAMPLE: *I would like to build my experience in the Catering industry as I enjoy cooking.*

EDUCATION /QUALIFICATIONS: (*State as per your supporting documentation*)

OTHER ACHIEVEMENTS: **EXAMPLE** (*Won a prize, wrote an article etc*)

REFEREES Nominate 3 people who know you and are willing to offer a verbal reference on your behalf. (Give name & where you know them from, plus add a daytime mobile contact number.)

2nd Page (include work history)

WORK HISTORY/WORK EXPERIENCE

EXAMPLE: (*worked part time for a fast food outlet - outline duties/ responsibilities)*

NAME OF ORGANIZATION / DATES WORKED THERE

KEY RESPONSIBILITIES:

NAME OF ORGANIZATION / DATE WORKED THERE

KEY RESPONSIBILITIES:

Chapter Four

Writing

Job Applications

It is important to show a professional image when applying for any position. Whether sending by mail or email, every aspect of your application will be scrutinized, ensuring it meets the requirements of the potential employer. A good application is an important step towards being offered an interview

If you only do half a job on your application, then an employer will feel that you will only do 'half a job' if they employ you. The acceptable format for an application is as follows.

Documentation supporting your application will be:

1. **Cover letter**, outlining why you are applying and what skills you can bring to the role.

2. An up to date **Resume**/CV (as detailed in the previous chapter).

3. Copies of **Qualifications** to support application.

4. If sending by email, a short message stating the documentation contained within the email.

Covering letter should be:

✓ Make the letter just one page, nobody wants to read pages and pages of information. By being concise and picking your sentences carefully, this should not be a problem.

✓ Keep to the point by addressing the selection criteria. If they ask for specific skills, then demonstrate your knowledge and/or experience in that area. If you have covered this in your Resume, give an overview in just one paragraph in the letter.

✓ It is essential that you use KEYWORDS in your application to reflect experiences listed in the Job Description. It appears that Government agencies and some companies are now using computer programs to analyze applications, picking up keywords of the position, eg communications skills, specific IT experience.

✓ Make sure the letter is neat and reads well. Language should be in full, no shortening of words or using numbers to replace letters. Don't assume that the person reading the letter can understand jargon or 'texting' language.

✓ Your opening sentence should state the position you are applying for and why you are interested in being considered.

✓ Final sentence should state, something like, "I look forward to hearing from you.

✓ Sign off should be: Yours sincerely
                                      John Brown or Susan Green

✓ Physically sign the letter. If sending by email, sign using an attractive font, say Times Roman, and italicize it. Attach Word document to email as it, don't save as a jpeg.

✓ It is important to 'file' all documents within your own electronic filing system, in a way that will allow you to find them easily. I suggest you set up a folder called Applications, and then create subfolders for each company you apply to. All documentation sent to each company can be filed separately using this system. It also keeps track of applications you have submitted, plus contact details of company representatives.

✓ I would include in that file a copy of the email you send to the company. Just open up the email message, click on File, and 'save as' into your file folder.

Each email should include a request for a 'read receipt', so that you are sure the intended recipient has received your application. It is useful if you need to follow up at any time to have these details to hand.

✓ If you are mailing your application, there can be no 'read receipt', so it is appropriate that after one week you ring the company to ensure they have received your application.

If you do this, make a note on your copy of the application that you did make the call, who you spoke to, and the response you received. Signature on a hard copy letter should be by hand as it is not appropriate to use an electronic signature on this occasion.

I have included a template letter you can use to apply for any position.

LETTER TEMPLATE

Name
Address
Phone No: Mobile
Email Address:

Insert Date:

Name of person applying to. Use Mr. Mrs. Ms

If sending by email, show email address

Dear ...Use Sir/Madam (*if you do not know name of contact person*)

I should like to apply for the position of .... as advertised in SEEK on date, and enclose my Resume, together with copies of my qualifications for your information.

I am interested in the position as I have been working with (*animals in the local Veterinary Clinic where I was accepted for Work Experience in October this year.   Elaborate on what you enjoyed.*

(If you had a position with any responsibilities, highlight what they were and how you managed the role. If you have a number of points to talk about, use dot points or another defining symbol).

To finish add a paragraph on what skills or attributes you can bring to the position eg you think strategically, or you are skilled at using certain computer programs etc etc. Don't forget to use KEYWORDS here

If you play in a team, although your resume will have these details, it doesn't hurt to talk about being a "team player', or a good communicator.

Final sentence should say something along the lines of:

I look forward to hearing from you.

Yours sincerely
If mailing make sure you sign your letter as it make it more personal (not electronic)

Signature
Full name

EMAIL COVER NOTE

When emailing an application, follow the instructions given by the company advertising.

✓ In the **SUBJECT LINE** of the email show the position title plus position number if applicable.

✓ Dear (name of person you have addressed the letter of application to)

✓ Content of email:
  Please find attached my application for the position of ………
  together with my Resume and copies of qualifications.

✓ Add you name and contact phone number underneath.

  John Smith
  0400.000.000

You do not need to recreate the information in your letter, this is just a brief note to say what documentation you are sending.

It is a good idea to add '**Request a Read Receipt**'. Find this under **Options** within the email you are sending.

APPLYING ON LINE

To make it easier to manage your letter of application using an online program, I suggest you type your letter as per the template instructions, and if possible 'cut and paste' into the box provided. If you are limited to a number of words, then work out what does not need to be included here, as it is covered in your Resume, which you will also have to attach.

Make the presentation of information, as neat and tidy as you can.

Chapter Five

Preparing

For Interview

Once you have secured an interview, it means that you have passed the first 'test' and therefore have an opportunity to 'sell' yourself face-to-face. The company is interested so this is where you need to shine.

✓ **Always** 'dress appropriately', first impressions are extremely important. This doesn't mean an expensive outfit, but it does mean it should be well laundered and ironed. For women if wearing a skirt or dress, although an old fashioned idea, stockings can complement an outfit.

   A 'tailored' jacket makes a great statement. If you don't own a jacket, have a look at a couple of second hand or retro stores, it is amazing the quality of some of their items. Choose something that suits your 'style' and looks presentable. It is easy to dry clean an item to give it a fresh new feel, and is reasonable cost effective.

✓ Think of your **whole** image, from head to toe.

✓ Makeup can be overdone, so be subtle if you are planning to wear any.

✓ Keep Jewellery to a minimum, especially bangles that constantly make a noise when you move, as it can distract the interviewer from listening to your responses.

✓ A coloured scarf can add a point of difference to a dark outfit.

✓ **Always** be who you are, don't try and act like someone else. Your personality is what needs to shine through, even though you may be nervous.

✓ **Be prepared.** You need to research the company, find out the background, what do they do, what is their philosophy. The company website will give you everything you need to know. It will give you confidence in answering questions when you have a feel for the business. You don't have to be an expert, but be aware of any new products or innovations they are currently working on.

✓ Did you receive a detailed **Job Description** when you applied for the position? More than not this would have been sent to you after your initial enquiry. You should have already studied this document, as your application should have addressed KEY duties and responsibilities. Have another look at the document and make sure you understand the role you are going to be interviewed about.

✓ As stated previously **you must look the part.** Dress for the position you want, **first impressions** are so important.

✓ **Always** turn up for an interview at least 15 mins early, which will give you time to let the nerves settle, and have a few quiet moments.

✓ **Always** be courteous to the receptionist, give your name and who you are there to see, plus the time of your appointment. NEVER underestimate the 'power' of the person at the front desk, as they may be asked their opinion of candidates being interviewed that day.

✓ **Always** turn OFF your mobile phone before approaching the receptionist, preferably before entering the office, and do not turn it on again until you have left the premises.

NOTES PAGE

CHAPTER SIX

THE INTERVIEW

It is a sign of good manners to shake hands with the Interviewer when you walk into the interview room. Make the handshake firm but not heavy or too weak.

If there is a panel, each person will ask you a question. When answering, address the person who has asked the question. This allows you to form a connection with each interviewer.

Sit upright, keeping your hands in your lap, **do not fidget**, or use wild hand movements. Ladies, if you are carrying a bag leave it by the chair, do not keep it on your lap. Smile, it may feel like an ordeal, but you need to show some level of confidence.

There is usually a glass of water provided for each candidate, so feel free to take a sip as and when you need to.

Do ask Questions when offered the opportunity to do so. This is usually done at the end of the interview. This gives you the opportunity to ask for clarification on something you were either unsure of, or would like further information.

Don't ask about Salary, or Entitlements, as it is not the time to do so. If you are offered the position, this information will be discussed at that time.

Be yourself, be confident, speak clearly, don't mumble. If you are unsure what is being asked, then ask them to restate it.
They know that you are nervous. Better to respond correctly, than offer something that has no relevance to the question.
When you get up to leave the room, just say thank you, get up and leave as directed by the interviewer.

TIP: When an interviewer asks how you are, as in "How are you today", it is just to make you feel at ease, so you don't need to return the question, which is something everyone seems to be doing these days.

Try not to 'waffle' in your answers. If you feel you have answered the question, then that is it, don't go off on tangents as this will detract from the answer. Be to the point in your answers, and if asked to elaborate a point, then think of a situation where you have been able to demonstrate the skill under discussion.

Interviewers know that candidates are nervous when they arrive, and they do their best to make you feel at ease, so that a strong conversation can occur between the two parties. If you feel you don't understand part of a question, you can ask them to rephrase or restate the information they are seeking. This is acceptable, however if you keep alert and make sure you are listening to what they are saying, this should not occur. Don't let your mind wander to other insignificant details.

Remember, this is your opportunity to shine.

Notes Page

CHAPTER SEVEN

POSSIBLE

INTERVIEW QUESTIONS

There are usually a select number of questions put to each candidate at interview. All candidates are asked the same questions so that a common level of assessment can be undertaken.

✓ **An introductory question may be to 'Tell us about yourself'** This is an opportunity to talk about your background, what you have been doing, studying, if this is your first job, then talk about your activities – sport, voluntary positions, education and qualifications.

✓ **Why do you think you are qualified for this position?** This is an important question where you need to sell yourself, and the qualities you feel you have to be successful in the position. Talk about your capabilities, what you are good at, and how those qualities will benefit the company. You must be clear on the answer and not 'waffle'.

✓ **Experience** Talk about relevant employment, community or educational experience. The type of industry you have worked in previously, the position you held and your level of responsibility at your previous place of work.

You will be asked how this experience relates to the current position. If this is your first job, then talk about what projects you have undertaken elsewhere, at TAFE or in voluntary positions or whatever experience you have that shows evidence of particular skills.

✓ **Why are you applying for the position?** This is where you talk about what is appealing about the position. It may be the type of industry or the type of work you will be undertaking. You may see it as an opportunity to get into a particular type of business that you are interested in. You may be asked to talk about longer term career aspirations. Be ready to discuss how you feel about the industry or position potential.

Remember, companies are looking for someone they can train into the company's way of operating. Someone who will turn up for work every day and do the best job they are capable of. They want someone who is a team player, works hard, whilst being of a personable nature.

The interview is an opportunity to show who you are, and showcase your credentials.

NOTES PAGE

Chapter Eight

Potential

Employers

You will be familiar with the various search engines available when looking for a job. It may be that you haven't really thought much about them until now.

The following are key sites worth looking at. Set up a login and complete the search fields to draw down on the type of position you would like to apply for. The system will generate an automatic response via email to you as and when a position appears to match your stated criteria.

1. **CAREERONE / SEEK** are similar sites, although Seek appears to be more broadly used by the public when searching for jobs. Take a look at both to make up your own mind.

2. **RECRUITMENT AGENCIES** – Go to Google and type in Job Seeker / Recruitment. Register with one or a few, this will get your name out there and it is amazing how much assistance these Agencies give candidates in finding a suitable position.

    NOTE: Nos 1 & 2 – both of these sites advertise positions where you are asked to apply 'on line'. Important issues to be aware of:

    -   Don't under value your application by sending in anything less than a full formal response.

    -   Read what the advert is asking you to do. Usually this will include sending your Resume and a Cover Note.

    -   Make sure you cover the position 'criteria', in respect to experience.

    -   Sometimes they provide a 'box' where you are supposed to write a letter. If that is the case, I would be using the template in Chapter 4, completing your letter in Word, then cut and paste into the space provided. You can use an electronic signature on this occasion.

- OR, if there is provision to upload documents, then ensure you have included these three essentials:
  - ✓ Covering Letter
  - ✓ Resume
  - ✓ Copy of Qualifications

3. **LINKEDIN** - It is worth setting up a profile here as it is a **professional site** and will connect you with a broad cross section of people, companies, all professional people looking to keep in touch. Become familiar with the type of information presented here, as it is aimed at a more businesslike profile than what you would put on your personal Facebook page.

4. **FACEBOOK** is purely a social site, however it is wise to keep information of a 'personal' nature limited to who can see it. It is now common practice for a company or recruitment agency to view your 'Facebook' page to get a feel for the person they are going to interview. Obviously if the language or photos are not in good taste, it may cost you a job opportunity. Take time to review who can see what on your site.

5. **USE YOUR NETWORKS** – Think about the people you know, the organizations or associations they belong to. What is happening in their world? It is amazing how many job opportunities come out of 'Who you Know'. When an opportunity arises, be proactive and lodge an expression of interest. It may be just the 'break' you are looking for.

6. **READ THE NEWSPAPER –** There will be plenty of information on companies who plan to expand their operations and will be looking to build their employee base.

7. **CAREERONE -** Keep abreast of the articles contained in this section of the newspaper, there are some terrific tips and tricks for understanding the necessary capabilities of being **WORK READY.**

NOTES PAGE

Chapter 9

Traineeships

&

Apprenticeships

Don't overlook the potential of undertaking either a:

- ✓ **Traineeship** – which is usually administratively based or
- ✓ **Apprenticeship** – which is usually Trades based position.

The type of job you are keen to pursue, will make the choice relatively easy.

Again check out the web for Australian Apprenticeships / Traineeships as there is a myriad of information that will assist you to work through the process of applying and the criteria for these positions.

I have seen Schools advertise Traineeships within their office, so jobs can be very close at hand, without ever realizing it. Wonderful is you need to work school hours.

Traineeships are usually a twelve month appointment, but there is always a chance that the employer, once having trained the trainee, will retain them and integrate them into their organization as a permanent employee.

Apprenticeships, depending upon the industry, can run for up to three to four years. Again after a person has completed their apprenticeship they would be fully qualified in their chosen trade, and will be a real asset to any company. Good Tradesmen are like 'hens teeth' there just aren't enough to go around.

Look at http://www.skills.sa.gov.au/apprenticeships-traineeships Which will give you all the information you require on Australian Apprenticeships / Traineeships.

The website states:
> *"Search for a career, see what training you need and get ready for the job you want. Get information about the employment prospects, qualifications that are linked to occupations, training pathways to get there and where to go for more information"*

Contact their office on the 'Infoline' 1800 506 266 for clarification on the information presented. Actively engage with the people who are there to help you work through the process.

CHAPTER TEN

BE ACTIVE, JOIN A

PROFESSIONAL

ASSOCIATION

It may seem that being unemployed, becoming a member of a professional association would not be an option open to you, as you are not currently part of the workforce.. This however this is not the case.

There would be a number of member based Associations that have special categories which would welcome new members. They have what is called 'Affiliate' membership which is aimed specifically at people who are still pursuing their career options.

Take a look on the Web, and type in 'Professional Associations' and see what comes up. For instance, if you are planning a career in office administration, the Australian Institute of Office Professionals (AIOP) is one you would consider.

Why Join a Professional Association? The connections made through membership are widespread. You meet people from a cross section of industries, all with varying levels of experience, who are keen to impart their knowledge to enthusiastic new members. This is a 'goldmine' for personal development. You never know who you are going to meet, but whoever it is, you will learn something from them. In saying that they may well learn something from you, due to your background and schooling. It is a win:win situation for everyone, and a 'safe' environment to get to know people.

There will be a cost of membership, though usually this is a special price for Associate members. Talk to the organization and say you are interested in joining, and if there are any special payment options available. Although the initial cost may appear 'expensive' at the time of joining think of it as an investment in your future and could well be the 'stepping stone' to future opportunities for your personal growth. With membership comes many specially reduced cost development opportunities, and will link you with other like-minded people.

Whether commencing or recommencing your career, the fact that you belong to a professional association will look great on your Resume, as it shows a company you are serious about your future. Get actively involved.

Chapter Eleven

The Value Of

Volunteering

The value of volunteering should not be under estimated.

Volunteers come from many different backgrounds and bring with them a myriad of life experiences. You find them in Hospitals, supporting key community services, eg Meals on Wheels, Charities, RSPCA, Society for the Blind. The list is endless and each and every volunteer makes their mark creating win:win situations for the organizations they support.

Volunteering is an amazing past time. It allows you to be involved in activities that would not normally come your way. You meet a myriad of people you wouldn't normally get to meet, that broadens your life experiences as you learn new skills.

My experience of being a volunteer was though a long involvement with the Australian Institute of Office Professionals. I joined in 1992 and never would have imagined that it would have led me in 2011 to become National President. What a journey it has been. I have met so many talented people and probably reinvented myself along the way, from being quite an introvert to actually being able to present at seminars and conferences.

Look for what you have a passion for, perhaps sports, continued learning, medicine, whatever it is look for organizations that need assistance. You will then be working within an environment that you feel strongly about which enhances 'job satisfaction'. It is a great start to a possible career move.

Volunteers also bring 'new blood' to an organization. With that comes new ideas which is invaluable as companies look to continue to be relevant in the fast paced world of technology.

So, if you feel you have the passion, take the first step and approach a company or organization of your choice. Ask to speak to a Human Resources representative, or if a smaller enterprise, the Manager. Let them know your background and what you feel you have to offer as a Volunteer. This could be the beginning of something wonderful, as you never know where this step will take you.

Being a Volunteer is a 'free' experience, plus if you are not as yet in the workforce, your time spent with any organization will keep you positive and motivated, as you connect with people working together for the benefit of others.

Volunteering is not just giving to others, it is time invested in yourself as you learn new skills and build relationships with other motivated people.

NOTES PAGE

CHAPTER TWELVE

NEVER, EVER

GIVE UP

Last but certainly not least, be kind to yourself as it may take time to find your 'dream' job. You should however look at any opportunity to get into the workforce as an interim step, as it will give you the gift of work experience, and open the door to a new environment where you meet people. This in itself builds confidence in who you are, and may well open the door to other possibilities.

Transitioning into the Workforce is not for the feint hearted, it takes time and effort to set the wheels in motion to achieve a positive outcome. But remember, the ball is very much in your court to make things happen. You are the catalyst that will make your transition successful.

If you take on board the points outlined in this booklet, you may well be on the way to finding a suitable position.

Where there is continued positivity, there will always be a positive outcome.

GOOD LUCK

ACTION LIST

ITEM	ACTION TO BE TAKEN	TICK BOX
1	Read the Book to reinforce information presented	
2	Create or update your Resume using templates provided	
3	Create your covering Letter of Application	
4	Create your electronic filing system for applications.	
5	Register online with SEEK / Careerone for positions that interest you.	
6	Check Wardrobe for Interview Outfit. Go Shopping – Be selective Check out Sales.	
7	Be Ready – practice answering Interview Questions	
8	Research Company before attending Interview	

THE AUTHOR

CATHERINE MIDDLETON

Catherine has been in the workforce for over 40 years, and in that time worked in a variety of Industries, both in the Private and Public Sector.

Her experience comes from holding a variety of positions where she has worked her way up the career ladder, before retiring from full time employment and setting up her own company,

OFFICE Dynamics Adelaide.

Catherine works with companies to ensure that their administrative operations are efficient and effective, by undertaking reviews and implementing strategies to align the business with best practice.

She was a volunteer for over 20 years in a not for profit, member based professional development organization, The Australian Institute of Office Professionals, where she held the position of National President / Chair of the Board of Directors from 2011-2013.

Her passion for assisting people to be the best they can be in their chosen profession, has seen her undertake a number of public speaking opportunities to promote ongoing career development.

Her interest in assisting the unemployed transition into the workforce, has seen the formation of a number of interactive workshops that assist in providing clear strategies when applying for positions and attending the all important interview. This handbook will therefore be invaluable to any job seeker in assisting them through the recruitment process.

Further information can be found at
www.officedynamicsadelaide.com.au

or copies can be purchased directly from
 https://www.createspace.com/6566294

www.ingramcontent.com/pod-product-compliance
Lightning Source LLC
Chambersburg PA
CBHW060230290526
45789CB00003B/1492